Quiet Water Kayaking
By
Leslie Dunn

D0062772

Printed in the United States of America
ISBN 978-0-9726998-3-9

This instructional guidebook is intended as an adjunct to hands-on training by professional or experienced kayakers. Participating in water-related sports is a personal choice of accepting full responsibility for one's own safety.

Chapter 1

Different Types of Kayaking

As an American Canoe Association certified kayak Instructor, I've taught hundreds of new kayakers. Classes begin with a group huddle during which we discuss paddling terminology, how to communicate on the water via Universal River Signals (described in Chapter 6), money saving tips on what to buy and not buy and basics about recreational kayaking. Of all the questions, only one is asked during every class: "What do I do when my boat flips?" During the first few classes I taught, we discussed best practices – blow three long blasts on the whistle attached to your PFD, float on your back and point your feet down river, etc.

Instead of the answer reassuring them, though, the fear behind the question seemed out of proportion to capsizes on recreational paddles.

Problem was I was too close to the issue. I related their question to an event that occurs repeatedly during group recreational paddles I'd led - boat flips, paddler swims or walks to the riverbank while the other paddlers grab gear floating downstream. Upon questioning them, my students explained that they imagined themselves pinned or trapped under their kayak, or floating out of control in a churning, boiling current and slamming into rocks. The problem was that I knew that kayaking comes in different flavors, but *they didn't*. Many of them thought kayaking meant paddling down rapid currents. Period.

Classes now begin with a brief explanation of the different types of kayaking and classification of waterways, that the day's lesson covers recreational paddling only and not the higher risk type of kayaking known as "whitewater." Always, several students sigh with relief, and relax.

I was curious what caused novice paddlers to think kayaking only meant the high thrill whitewater stuff.

"The Olympics."

Oh.

"YouTube."

Oh, that, too.

"The news."

It's a wonder any of them showed up for class.

Water Classifications

The classification of waterways known as "The International Scale of River Difficulty" enables paddlers worldwide to speak the same language regarding water current. Waterways are categorized on a scale of I-VI, with I being the slowest and easiest to maneuver and VI "impossible" to navigate. A Class I river in Florida has the same characteristics as a Class I river in Germany.

Recreational paddling, the subject of this book, occurs in Class I-II current. Only recently has Class VI earned a new description from "impossible to kayak" to "unraftable" - leave it to fellow kayakers with never-say-die verve earning Class VI this new perspective.

Class I represents the most obstacle-free bodies of water such as lakes and lazy rivers. This classification is this book's subject matter. Unless you live where the terrain is flat, please be prepared for a few challenging (read: scary) sections on even Class I rivers. Those stretches of river that require skill, experience and muscle are called "technical." There is nothing technical about the following photo:

Class II, in the following photo, requires a bit more skill to navigate boulders, drops of the terrain, downed trees and other challenges.

Waterways change from one classification to another dependent on rainy seasons. For days after a severe storm, a creek with no more than a trickle of water transforms into a bank overflowing Class II.

Patches of difficult runs sometimes qualify adding the symbols "+" or "-" to that river's river classification. The photo on the following page is an example of a Class II with a section that is not quite Class III but definitely Class II+:

Whitewater classification begins with Class III. Paddlers *must* know how to self-rescue, perform rolls with confidence and have advanced paddling skills to navigate rapids, standing waves, rocks and boulders.

Olympic events are performed in Class III-IV whitewater or, the more easily remembered descriptive name, "wildwater."

Class IV waterways are boiling, frothy, raging rivers and the highest class most kayakers attempt to paddle. Most violent and dangerous are Class V and Class VI currents.

In my neck of the woods, 'whitewater' is the preferred term by Class III, and higher, paddlers. Whitewater earned its name from the frothy bubbles generated by turbulent water. On national on-line message boards, paddlers type "WW" as an abbreviation homogenizing the difference between the terms white- and wildwater.

TIP: Stick to Class I waterways to learn to kayak.

Types of Kayaking

Recreational: Recreational kayaking is the fastest growing type of paddling. There simply are more available waterways at this level. The slower pace offers more opportunity for viewing wildlife and scenery, is age and gender neutral meaning boys and girls about age eight through eighty enjoy it, and combines fun with a great workout.

Class I offers smooth, easy paddling. You may encounter gentle winds blowing across a lake that take effort to keep the boat moving in a straight line or some tricky bends on a river; nothing that demands a great deal of skill. Class II differs from Class I in that you *will* encounter situations that require skill such as "strainers" which are downed trees that spans across the water and pulls the current (and you!) toward it, "drop offs" where the terrain suddenly lowers in elevation causing the water to rush; and "riffles" or "swifts" which are sections of shallow fast flowing water over a stretch of rocks. If the wind across the lake increases in velocity and causes whitecaps, the lake graduates from Class I to Class II.

Due to the higher degree of safety, recreational paddling in Class I water is one of the few sports in which families can participate together. Paddle with a group or with a partner. Lots of paddlers even bring their dog.

Another reason for the popularity of recreational kayaking is the affordable cost. Recreational kayaks range from $200 for a no frills floating barge to an elite kayak priced at $700+. Compare this to whitewater kayaks, the cost of which can be twice the cost of an elite recreational kayak. Purchase a PFD (Personal Flotation Device) and a paddle and for a total of $500 to $1,000 you are set up for years of kayaking fun.

Recreational kayaking offers multiple outdoor adventures. Fish in weedy spots inaccessible to larger watercraft, paddle primitive sections of rivers too shallow for motorboats or glide near wildlife for great photographs. ⌐ıı a tent, a change of clothes, food and water ın your boat and go river camping.

River campers float, for instance, ten to fifteen miles, camp overnight on the riverbank and then paddle the rest of the trip to the 'take-out,' the place where the car awaits. This requires a little preplanning to get the cars where they need to be. Several friends of mine travel to South Florida for an annual inexpensive vacation river camping every year during the week between Christmas and New Years.

Whitewater (aka 'Wildwater'): Beginning with Class III, whitewater beckons to the more adventurous, experienced paddler. Key word: Experienced! Before heading out for the challenge, please have more than a few Class I and Class II paddles under your PFD. Then prepare by learning from an experienced instructor or whitewater enthusiast self-rescue techniques such as Eskimo rolls, wet exits and how to rescue paddling buddies. Learn how to be rescued, too! Rolls, which require lots of practice, upright the kayak with a snap of the hip and during a wet exit a paddler leaves the flipped kayak and swims to safety.

In the slower waters of Class I, paddlers easily assist one another when anyone flips their boat. Assisting others in Class II is more challenging and rescue practice is recommended. In Class III and higher, self-rescue and group rescue training is a must. ACA and other paddle sport organizations offer courses that teach effective rescue methods and highly recommended for whitewater paddlers. A reliable roll, experienced whitewater paddling buds trained in rescues, and the best PFD (Personal Flotation Device – life jacket) and helmet you can afford are absolute necessities.

None of this is meant to scare anyone from doing Class III+. For the daredevils and adrenaline junkies, the above paragraphs may even entice you. Since this book's audience is paddling novices, understanding the difference between whitewater and recreational paddling especially as it applies to safety is crucial.

Now for the whitewater fun: Skimming along the current, flipping and then righting your kayak, a challenge as accessible as the nearest run, testing your limit, reading the water, ferrying across the river, eddy hopping - it makes doing 3.7 seconds on a bull named Foo Man Choo nothing more than a warm up exercise!

Ocean (aka 'Surf'): Ocean and fishing kayaking are close seconds as the fastest growing type of kayaking. Companies pump money into engineering new and better designs of ocean kayaks for three reasons: In the world of sports ocean kayaking is new (began in the '70's compared to kayaking in general that is thousands of years old), folks that hang out at the beach generally have more disposable income, and the multiple opportunities for fun that ocean kayaking offers such as fishing or riding the waves.

Nearly every type of kayak has an ocean counterpart. For example, short sea kayaks appear similar to whitewater boats, and long ones appear similar to touring kayaks. At a glance, I cannot determine the difference between a river and ocean sit on top and can imagine hooking a big one in the ocean means a hootin' and hollerin' free ride until the fish tires and then pulled onto the deck.

Sit on tops provide extra balance by the nature of its design and have less of a learning curve than other kayaks. They look like floating waffles. When you capsize, flip the boat over, climb back on and the water drains through the scupper holes which are openings on the deck. The kayaks similar to whitewater and touring kayaks require more equipment and advanced skills.

If riding waves beckon, consider the new "waveski," an elite breed of kayak that come equipped with fins, footstraps, seat and seatbelt.

Creeking: Most similar to whitewater but different enough to deserve its own classification. What we generally see of creeks are meandering thin ribbons of flowing water that add selling points to a home owner's property description. However, due to their narrow channels, it takes one good rainstorm to turn the meandering ribbon into a widened swath of torrential flow. Expect sudden drops and crops of rocks that require so much boat navigating hip action that it would make a belly dancer jealous. As with whitewater kayaking, purchase a helmet and PFD as though your life depended on it.

There are kayaks specifically designed for creeking.

Touring (aka 'Expedition'): You may want to consider touring kayaking if the thought of paddling long stretches of water and camping along the banks of a river sounds appealing. Some of these types of kayaks used in the ocean are the longest and narrowest of kayaks requiring expert balance and roll maneuvers.

John Guider, author of *"A River Inside,"* set off in his backyard creek near Nashville, Tennessee with not much more than his canoe and, at his friend's insistence, an axe. By the end of three months he paddled all the way to New Orleans. He returned home (by land) with the seed of his book, amazing photographs and the desire to do it again. Although Mr. Guider experienced his adventure in a canoe, a touring kayak would work just as good.

Getting away from it all motivates many touring paddlers. Think of the kayak as a floating cabin in which is stored everything needed for overnighters.

Please take a really good first aid kit and know how to use it since you'll be on your own miles from civilization where cell phones towers often do not reach. Better yet, take a buddy. Touring kayaks are most similar to recreational kayaks. The differences will be covered in Chapter 3.

Slalom racing: An Olympic event, literally. Competitive slalom kayaking (and canoeing) events are performed in whitewater Classes III+, whitewater boats and timed.

Other forms of kayaks include pedal, multi-hull and, the new kid on the block, hybrid boats that blend features of a kayak and canoe sometimes called a kay-oe.

Chapter 2

Recreational Terms and Slang

Bilge pump - Used to remove unwanted water from inside the boat. The best ones simultaneously suck up and propel the water over the edge of the boat. "Super soakers" children water squirt guns will do the job, and sponges sop up excess drips and small puddles.

Boat camping - Similar in meaning to "car camping" such that the words 'boat' and 'car' denote method of transporting the gear, and not the venue of the campsite. Boat camp on public islands or riverbanks. Canoes and touring kayaks provide ample storage space to stash camping supplies. Recreational kayaks of almost any size can be outfitted to carry minimum camping needs – sleeping bag, change of clothes and food.

Bow – Front end of the boat

Broached – See *"Pinned"*

Bulkhead - An upright wall behind the seat. Either built, or added as an option, into a kayak. Strongly recommended for recreational paddlers.

Coaming – Curled down rim around the cockpit over which a sprayskirt is attached. Provides a means to grab the boat for lifting it, exits, etc.

Deadfall – Natural debris in the river such as trees.

Divorce kayak – (slang) A tandem, two seater boat. For boaters who understand that the person in front sets the lead for strokes, and that the person in back does the steering, this term does not apply. If, however, two people paddling together results in banging each other's paddles while making little progress in the forward movement through the water, or worse flips, then this humorous term applies.

Drops – Where the land's elevation slopes down resulting in rushing downhill water. On approach, drops sound like waterfalls.

Drybag – Bags of varying material, size and quality made specifically to keep things inside of it dry. On a small and economical scale, small plastic bags that seal airtight are drybags. Drybags with flat bottoms enable standing them upright. Fold the top down twice then clip, snap or buckle it shut. Leave air inside when closing it to provide buoyancy in the event of a capsize.

Edging – A polished method of making the boat glide around a curve. Although one can edge while recreational kayaking, it is primarily a whitewater term that refers to the act of slightly tilting the boat downward by pushing down one hip, thigh or knee.

Emergency blanket – Metal-covered shiny thin plastic that comes in a small pouch that opens to the size of a shower curtain. Reflects body heat back to the person. Used for hypothermia, shock. If a paddler capsizes and the air or water, or both, are cold, don't wait until the paddler starts shaking to take action. Remove the paddler's wet clothes, get them into dry clothes and wrap them in the blanket.

Feathered – Refers to angling paddle blades 45, 60 or 90 degrees. Most recreational paddling is done with the blades straight up and down. When paddling in the wind, however, an angled blade slices through the breeze. I recommend purchasing a paddle with adjustable blades.

Life Jacket – See *PFD*

Long boat - (slang) A recreational kayak.

Long boaters – (slang) A term used by whitewater paddlers to differentiate their flavor of kayaking from those who paddle recreational kayaks.

Noodle arms – (slang) Worn out and sore arm muscles for a couple days after the paddle.

Paddle – Used as a verb (Let's go paddle!), noun (Put your paddle in the water). Add an "r" to the end and it becomes a common noun (Are you a paddler?).

Paddle float – Also known as 'outrigger.' Flotation devices that encase paddle blades for the purpose of balancing the boat. A paddle float balances a kayak in much the same way that training wheels balance a bicycle. Paddle floats can also be purchased that do not attach to the paddle blade but, instead, attach to the boat as a separate device. Used for rescues, to balance a boat while fishing or to create a 'barge" kayak for camping.

Paddle leash – A stretchy cord that, with one end clipped onto the boat and the other end slipped around the paddle, tethers the paddle to the boat to prevent paddle loss.

Pillow – Water flowing downstream over a rock. On approach, it could look like a good place to paddle over but it is not. Generally a whitewater term.

Pinned (also called *"Broached*) – A dangerous situation where a boat gets trapped against an obstacle such as a tree, debris or rock. Pinning often results in a crushed and/or submerged kayak. If you cannot *immediately* free the boat, get out and abandon the boat. This is a life and death situation.

Point – The lead paddler of a group experienced enough to read the water, look out for potential danger spots and scout best navigation on the waterway. All other paddlers stay behind the point. If there are experienced canoeists among the group, their higher elevation in the water as opposed to kayaks makes them ideal to be the point paddler.

Portage – The physical act of walking your boat. Perhaps the water is too low to float the kayak, an object such as a low lying tree blocks the river or the current is too dangerous or beyond the paddler's experience level. Note: pronounced "por tedge" or 'por tahj'"

Put in – A spot where paddlers begin a paddle, often at a bridge.

Rack – (slang) Short for 'roof rack.'

Rec – Short for 'recreational' kayak, as in, "Nice rec kayak.'

Recreational kayak – Most defining features is the large cockpit. Range in size from eight to fourteen feet. Built for stability and, in the higher price range, comfort and good tracking. Disadvantages: Longer boats do not take curves as good as shorter boats. Inexpensive rec boats put paddlers at risk when confronting dangerous river conditions such as strong currents and strainers. (See *"Strainers"*)

Riffles – A short stretch of the river characterized by shallow water and tons of small rocks and boulders. The water looks sparkly or bubbly as it runs over these rocks. The danger of riffles is the sudden increased water velocity.

Generally, riffles can be seen and not heard, as opposed to drops which can be heard on approach.

Roll – A whitewater term referring to the act of righting a kayak after a capsize. For example: Eskimo roll. Recreational kayaks are not made for rolls, although possible in a short one (eight foot) in which the rider's hips touch both sides and the boat skirted. (see *"Skirt"*)

Rudder – A device that, like a dog's tail, flips up over the back of the boat (stern) and lowers into the water, the movement of which is controlled by the paddler's feet. It's usually an added purchase for a kayak. The rudder assists with keeping the boat moving straight or as a passive use for rounding curves using the current's momentum. It saves energy as the paddler does not have to use as much effort to keep the boat moving straight. It's recommended for windy lakes, deep rivers and ocean paddles. Caution: Remember to flip the rudder onto the boat when encountering shallow water.

Run – (slang) Synonym for the verb 'paddle': "We're going for a run on the river."

Run the chute – (slang) As the result of obstructions, rocks for instance, in rivers of classes II+, paddlers confronted with a downstream narrowing of the flow must decide which path to take. The decision begins with a few minutes of holding the kayak still in the water, or scanning from the land, for the best place to 'run the chute.'

SOT – Abbreviation for sit-on-top kayak

Sculling – Moving the paddle in the water in a figure '8'. Used to maintain stability or as a drawstroke to move the boat sideways or by whitewater paddlers to resurface a capsized kayak.

Self-bailing – This does not refer to the paddler as the 'self' in self-bailing. It refers to a feature of the boat; more specifically to sit-on-tops kayaks. 'Scupper' holes span the width of the boat to allow water to drain through the boat.

Self-rescue – Depending upon one's self for uprighting and re-entry; most often associated with kayaking Class III+ bodies of water.

Shuttle, non-shuttle paddle – On a shuttle paddle the put-in and take-out are geographically distant from one another. Beginning at one bridge on a river and paddling downstream ten miles is an example of a shuttle paddle. Shuttle paddles require at least two vehicles as one is left at the beginning location of the paddle and the other vehicle at the stopping point of the paddle. Some facilities, state parks and outfitters offer shuttling. Lone paddlers can do nonshuttle paddles as the put-in and take-out are at the same location. Paddling upriver x number of miles, then drifting back down is an example of a nonshuttle paddle.

Skeg – With the kayak suspended, turned sideways and the skeg down, it looks like a tongue sticking down from the bottom of the boat pointing toward the back of the boat (stern). Some are built in and some are retractable. Its use is compensating for the wind rather than tracking, a definite plus for lake and sea kayaking.

Skirt – An apparel/device that effectively seals one's body to a whitewater kayak for the purpose of preventing water from entering the boat. Used with Class III+. It is important that the skirt fits snugly around the paddler's midsection. For recreational kayaks, half skirts are available that fit around the front half of the cockpit (only) decreasing the size of the cockpit by fifty percent in the event of rain or turbulent water.

Sit-on-top – Also known as *sit upons*. Used for recreational, whitewater and sea kayaking. Advantages: easy to mount as there is no cockpit to climb inside, foot rests molded into the boat, scupper holes for self-draining, after a capsize paddler flips boat and climbs back on, full open deck allows for more gear storage.

Disadvantages: Some have no back rest, paddler stays in same seated position for duration of trip, higher center of gravity resulting in less stability (does not apply to all sit-on-tops, some manufacturers compensate with additional width or lower seats), generally slower moving than sit insides.

Swamped – A water-filled kayak.

Sweep – The last person paddling downstream in a group paddle. All other paddlers remain in front of the sweep paddler. The sweep should be the strongest and most experienced paddler. Sweeps are in the best position to swoop downstream to assist with a capsize. Did you tip your sweep today?

Swimmer – (slang) Also called "Floater." Navy folks would call out, "Man overboard!" A swimmer is a capsize victim.

Take out – The end location of a paddle.

Tandem – Boat with two or more seats. Recreational, touring, whitewater and sit-on-tops are available as tandems.

Technical – Paddlers use this term to describe a waterway, or a section of a waterway, that requires skill and muscle to navigate as in, "It's a technical river." Or "There's a couple technical stretches to paddle."

Touring kayak – Made for excellent tracking and to traverse long distances. The length enables plenty of stowing space for camping equipment as these boats are the longest kayaks.

Tracking – How straight the boat stays with each paddle stroke. Good tracking = the boat stays straight. Bad tracking = the boat points first in one direction then the other with each stroke. The best determining factor for tracking is length. The longer the boat, the better it tracks. An 8' boot cannot compare to a 12' boat for tracking while neither compares to a 17' touring kayak.

WW – paddler's abbreviation for whitewater or wildwater

Yak – (slang) Kayak

Note: This list is not comprehensive, and lists primarily terms found in this book for recreational kayakers.

Chapter 3

Types of Boats

In the broadest sense, there are two types of kayaks: sit inside and sit on top.

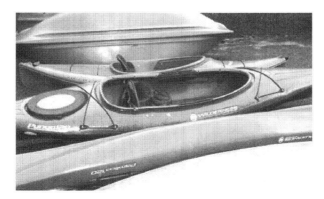

Sit Inside

Sit on Top, also called Sit Upon

Recreational: While many paddlers use sit on tops for recreational kayaking, for the purpose of this book let's agree that recreational kayaking is done in sit inside kayaks.

A defining feature of a recreational kayak is the large opening for the cockpit (the hole you slip inside to sit in the boat) as opposed to the much smaller opening found on a touring kayak. That's how to tell at a glance whether the boat is a recreational or touring kayak. A recreational river paddler's best friends are weight (of the boat) and length. Recreational boats range from eight to fourteen feet in length, and from thirty-two to seventy plus pounds. Avoid the low and high ranges of these lengths and weights. Most paddlers find that the perfect length for recreational kayaks is ten to twelve feet with a weight in the forties. Choose a twelve foot boat for a more stability, if you need to carry more things than the average paddler or are taller than six feet.

If the boat is too light with a weight in the thirty-something pound range, it floats more on top of the water and is less stable. Imagine putting a plastic bowl in a swimming pool. The bowl easily rocks back and forth, and with a light flick of the wrist the bowl swirls around. In terms of being on a river, that flick of the wrist mimics the action of a good wind or the current. Now imagine a heavier soup bowl in the pool. It sits deeper in the water as it isn't as buoyant as the lighter plastic and doesn't rock around nearly as much. Kayaks that weigh at least forty pounds displace more water than lighter boats thus adding secondary stability.

Durability is another issue. Consider that the difference between a thirty-two pound and a forty-five pound boat is thirteen pounds of whatever material of which theboat is made. The denser and thicker the boat, the longer it stands up to gouges, dings and dragging.

Bottom line: The shorter and lighter recreactional boats are less stable and durable than longer and heavier ones. For ladies concerned about carrying a longer and heavier boat, we'll cover tips in Chapter 5 how to load and unload a kayak.

Rule of thumb: The wider the boat, the more stable it is. For comparison, the long pencil-thin boats you may have seen racing

are twenty-three inches wide while a good-sized rec is twenty-seven inches wide.

The narrow touring boats are 'tippy' while the wider recs are more stable. However, the downside of wider *short* kayaks is decreased tracking. Ten to twelve feet recreational kayaks compensate nicely for both stability and tracking.

TIP: I once paddled a thirty inch wide boat and continually banged the paddle against the sides because it was just too wide to clear with each stroke. If you are really tall (6'3"+) choose a longer than average paddle (240 cm) rather than a wider boat.

Another factor that has an adverse effect on stability is if the seated paddler's hips span the width of the boat. If the paddler is too full in the seat, each wiggle of the paddler's behind causes rocking, unstable movements of the kayak. For whitewater paddling, that is the goal. For recreational paddling, that doesn't work. We need to be able to move inside our kayaks without our boat responding. If a paddler's butt is up against the sides of the boat, simply turning the torso, for example, to turn the kayak would cause the boat to dip down to the water. Not good.

With recreational kayaking, good tracking is everything. Here's the definition for tracking from Chapter 2:

"Tracking – How straight the boat stays with each paddle stroke. Good tracking = the boat stays straight.
Bad tracking - the boat points first in one direction then the other with each stroke. The best determining factor for tracking is length. The longer the boat, the better it tracks. An eight foot boat cannot compare to a twelve foot boat for tracking while neither compares to a seventeen foot touring kayak."

A river paddler in an eight foot boat expends energy in two ways: correcting with *each stroke* the direction the boat points while simultaneously moving the boat forward. I've seen an eight foot boat exhaust a toned paddler during a ten mile trip while others in ten to twelve foot boats had no problem. Paddling a boat too short for the job leads to fatigue.

Other than the large opening of the cockpit, eight to thirteen foot range of length and widths, there are no other statements that purely define a recreational kayak.

TIP: Low end boats often have an uncomfortable, butt numbing molded seat. Bring a stadium cushion.

Touring: Here are some unique features of a touring kayak: length range of fourteen to eighteen feet, small diameter cockpit, streamlined bow and stern.

EpicKayaks.com

These boats cut through the water as effortlessly as possible because their owner intends to cover long distances, reach top speed, or both. Watching someone glide across a large lake in a touring kayak is like watching music in motion. With the wind at their back, these paddlers zip along the water almost as fast as sailboats.

Synonymous words for touring kayaks is expedition and sea kayaks. An expedition tour might be a daylong or overnight excursion or a week of river camping. Due to the greater lengths, these boats offer more hatches, deck rigging and space to stash things like tents, sleeping bags, change of clothing and food.

Whitewater: When I first saw a whitewater kayak, I thought it looked like a large Dutch wooden shoe:

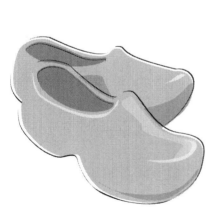 

Whitewater boats are "outfitted" which means that padding is added to snugly fit the boat to the paddler. The net effect is that the whitewater boat becomes an extension of the paddler's body.

Tim Rideout

The more of a person's body surface that touches the boat via outfitting, the more effectively the boat maneuvers.

Simply pressing down with one leg or hip turns these responsive boats. Also, pushing down with one hip lowers the boat on that side during the turn. The term for this is "edging."

In whitewater, capsizing is the norm, which makes quick, effective and reliable rolls critical. With a sharp left or right upward jerk of the butt, a "hip snap," the boat responds with a thrust to right itself. Permitting as little water as possible to get inside the boat is just as critical. To prevent water from getting inside the boat, whitewater boaters wear "skirts." The skirt fits snugly over the lip, or "coaming," of the cockpit. A grab tab is attached to the front of the skirt.

When placing the skirt over the coaming, it is essential that the grab tab sticks out. If a paddler is unable to perform an effective roll, a quick yank on the grab tab frees the skirt from the coaming and the kayaker performs a "wet exit." Gravity pulls the paddler out of the boat just as it would anything in an overturned boat. With a thrust of their legs against the bottom of the boat, the whitewater paddler, wearing the skirt, clears the boat and swims to safety.

Special Note: Do not take a recreational kayak into Class III+ river. Recreational kayaks can be used for Class I and Class II only, and I say Class II with reluctance. I do not recommend any recreational kayak over ten feet for Class II. Whitewater paddling must be done in a kayak designed specifically for whitewater.

Whitewater kayaks function opposite to that of recreational boats. Here are some of the general differences:

Whitewater	Recreational
Eight feet and less	Eight feet and longer
Built to recover easily from a capsize	Built for stability
Snugger fit the better	Boat wider than paddler
Built-in flotation	Purchased extra
Ideal for quick turning	Shaped to go straight

What about taking a whitewater kayak down a Class I or II river? It's just not a good idea as it exhausts the paddler. What makes it exhausting? Tracking. Think of watching a duck walk away from you. His butt waddles first one way and then the other. That is bad tracking.

These short six- to eight foot whitewater boats perform as designed by responding to each stroke pointing left with a stroke on the right side and then pointing right with a stroke on the left. Conversely in a recreational boat with good tracking, the boat stays straight with each stroke.

As stated earlier and worth repeating: In recreational kayaking, good tracking is everything. This is a defining difference between recreational and whitewater kayaking.

Inflatables: There are so many from which to choose, and at alluring prices. The cheapies cost $100 or less. More durable ones cost over $1,000. When browsing ads, to avoid inadvertently purchasing an inflatable please read the ad thoroughly! Some advertisers bury the word 'inflatable' in the boat description or even avoid the word. Here's an example of a deliberately vague inflatable kayak ad:

"Performance Travel Kayak.... Inflatable seats with adjustable support backrest and mesh pocket." No kayak has inflatable seats except inflatable kayaks. Inflatables are great additions to camping or bike trips because they can be folded up and stored for a short run. A family can purchase several for the cost of one hard-shell kayak. For a brief three mile paddle on a Class I river, an inflatable is adequate.

Now for the downside of inflatables with regard to recreational kayaking. With a wind or water current of anything more than low velocity, an inflatable spins in circles on top of the water. The air inside of it keeps it buoyant and, unless there is some hefty weight inside, it stays on the top of the water like a piece of foam.

Inflatables have little to no tracking ability. Paddlers told me that it feels as if the boat has a mind of its own; most strokes will be spent correcting the direction the boat is taking. I have seen a couple exceptions: a tandem inflatable with two riders who provided enough weight to counteract the inflatable's buoyancy, and a high end inflatable made of heavy enough material and with a metal spine that lowered the boat into the water such that it provided traction. When an inflatable springs a leak, the inflatable kayak will be where? On the water. The repair process: Dry the boat. Patch the hole. Dry the patch. On one paddle, a member had three leaks. Thirty-five people waited an hour with each of the three repairs. On another run, a paddler literally floated in circles in the mild, two mile per hour current. Mid-way through the paddle, the exhausted newbie deflated her boat and hopped into someone's canoe. She later said that she had noodle arms for a couple days.

Tandem: A boat with two seats instead of one. Most boats can be purchased as tandems. Tandems are an option for those with a paddle partner or who need an extra seat for a child, pet or gear. Two people who tandem in synch can easily outdistance a solo boat. On a non-shuttled river paddle with half of the run going with and the other half against the current, it's advantageous to have two people who can trade off paddling to prevent fatigue. On the down side, that added seat means extra length and weight. Generally, expect the sixty-pound range and higher for a recreational tandem boat.

It is sad that these boats have earned the nickname, "Divorce Kayaks." Two people who repeatedly clack paddles and navigate themselves into the bushes rather than going downstream are not having fun. The fix is simple. The rear paddler synchronizes strokes with the front paddler, and the rear paddler's role is that of being the boat's rudder. The person up front cannot see the person in the back, that's why it is up to the rear paddler's to synch up strokes with the front paddler. When the rear paddler matches the front paddler's strokes, the boat zings through the water effortlessly. I know. I've tried to keep up with them.

One other important thing in *any* two seater boat is that the heavier person sits in the back.

Sit on top (SOT) or Sit Upons: The advantages of a SOT are: self-draining through the use of "scupper holes"; in the event of a capsize SOT's are more easily climbed onto as opposed to sit-insides; and stability such that one can stand up while floating on the water. To enhance stability, sit-on-tops are either narrow with a very low seat or wide with a high seat. Because of the open deck, paddlers with limited flexibility or long legs feel less confined on a sit on top. A lengthy sit-on-top outfitted for fishing is a beautiful thing to see with plentiful netted pockets, built-in rod holders, deck rigging, straps and hatches – everything the fisherman needs within arm's length. Snap that wiggling fish up onto the deck. You couldn't do that in a sit-inside without getting fish whacked.

On the beach, you'll see paddlers on sit-on-tops riding the waves along with the surfers or far from the shore for some fishing. Disadvantages: Back strain after prolonged sitting, water coming up onto the deck through the scupper holes. For more, please see "Sit on Top" in Chapter Two.

Chapter 4

Buying a boat

And Paddling Related Equipment

With so many makes and models of kayaks on the market, selecting one is like going into a pet store for a puppy. Unless you know what you want, your decision may be based on emotion rather than information. Beginning your kayak years in your own boat gives you the advantage of matching your growing style to the specifications of your kayak, but please ask several seasoned paddlers for advice before the purchase.

At the risk of sounding corny, revealing flaws or shortcomings about one's boat is like ratting on a best friend. Paddlers quickly adapt their style and technique to their boat so what may have been a shortcoming at first is no longer an issue after a couple runs. For example, my twelve foot boat may have been a bit difficult to whip around bends when I first started paddling but I learned to compensate by anticipating the bend sooner rather than later and no longer consider it an issue. The boat's length provides extra stability, a factor of greater importance to river paddlers than quick turning.

When students decide to purchase a kayak they ask which one is the most versatile, meaning, which kayak can do it all? Sorry to say that there is no such thing. A whitewater boat is as different from a touring boat as a race car from a SUV. To shoe horn a boat into something other than for which it is made compromises the boats performance and the paddler's enjoyment.

When shopping for a boat, here are the primary considerations:
• What type of body of water will you paddle?
• Slow or fast current?
• How often you will kayak – twice a month, twice a season, twice a year?
• How important is the longevity of the boat?
• How much can you afford to spend?

River? Lake? Ocean? – Different boats for different strokes

Generally speaking, lake paddling is a paddle of solitude. Recreational paddlers often paddle with groups. Whitewater pits man against the force of nature - that's as far as I dare categorize kayakers.

Perhaps by now you may have a better understanding of the type of kayaking which interests you the most. For the rest of the text referring to boat purchase, this brief list will apply:

Lakes: Length is the key, up to nineteen feet with the average at sixteen feet. These are the longest boats in the kayaking family.

Class I-II: A blend of length (ten to twelve feet) and width (twenty-five to twenty-eight inches)

Class III+: Whitewater kayaks only – six to eight feet long.

Overnighters: Length again, but not to the extreme as for lakes. Fourteen to seventeen feet in length; the average touring kayak is sixteen feet long.

Ocean: Sit on tops ranging from eight to fourteen feet; also whitewater boats

Honestly – how often will you kayak?

It's premature to ask how often you will kayak if you haven't yet set foot in one. You will know within your first three to five paddles whether or not it's the sport for you.

Renting or borrowing first is a great idea. If outfitters are available in your area, when renting request a kayak of different length and manufacturer with each run. Join a paddle group and ask to borrow boats from members. If they are true paddlers, they will loan boats free of charge.

TIP: When money exchanges hands, it is not borrowing. It is renting and carries the risk of potential legal issues.

There may be a good reason you cannot own a kayak such as a shortage of storage space. Check if a friend or relative will share a spot in their yard or cellar/basement. Kayaking in your own boat is absolutely the way to go. In the long run it is worth it to invest an extra couple hundred for a higher quality boat with extra features, especially a cup holder and a padded adjustable seat.

Or you may try kayaking and decide yes, I like it but it's not the best thing I've ever done. If that's the case, don't purchase the cheapest barge out there or the few trips in it will only strengthen your resolve to end your paddling days. When manufacturers go for inexpensive it is at the expense of maneuverability and comfort and could turn your lukewarm feelings for paddling into downright dislike. The least expensive boats are the most stable but are miserable at tracking, and are uncomfortable. If you won't paddle a whole lot, at least go for the bottom line recommendations for each type of kayaking mentioned in the list above, or rent from a local outfitter.

How long will a kayak last?

Two words on which to focus are care and cost. You can purchase a less expensive craft and prolong its usage with good care and, conversely, purchase a more expensive boat but without good care shorten its longevity.

To ensure the longevity of your boat, purchase a boat designed for your favorite kind of kayaking. If you live where the river bottoms are sandy or most of your paddling will be on a lake, consider purchasing a fiberglass boat. That medium drives up the cost but is long lasting and lightweight. If, however, you live where the rivers are rocky, fiberglass will break. Fiberglass (and Kevlar) boats can be repaired but it's more fun to have your boat in the water than in the repair shop. For bodies of water with rocky bottoms, choose a thicker and durable material such as Rotomold (Rotationally Molded) plastic. Imagine peeling a potato. Those long curls of skin resemble the gouging effect of going over rocks. Unfortunately rocks are unavoidable for river paddlers in many states.

TIP: For boat repairs, check with a boat supply store to see if they repair yaks. They will either need to know what your boat is made of, or transport your boat to them so they can determine the kayak's compositional material. Some manufacturers sell patch kits comprised of the same material as the boat for do-it-yourself repairs.

Even when used for the purpose for which they are designed, kayaks take a beating. Sometimes they have to be dragged from the car to the put in or up a cement boat ramp, across rocky river bottoms when the water is low or portaged through the woods around a dam.

TIP: When transporting from the car to the water without assistance, from paddle to paddle alternate dragging the boat from the stern and bow. Despite continued bilging, water kept collecting inside my yak during a winter paddle. I asked the group to pull over so I could check it out. I discovered a nasty long gash in the bottom of the stern, the result of eight years of pulling the boat by bow only. Still, a dinged, scratched up kayak (read: well loved) beats a pristine shiny boat that rarely gets wet.

Let's say you are considering purchasing a ten feet long, thirty-two pound kayak that costs $200. At this length, weight and price, the frame can be bent. With moderate paddling at twice a month, this is a one season kayak. At the risk of sounding scary, that one season might not be a safe one for reasons discussed in Chapter 7.

It's reasonable for a top grade kayak to last five years or more with good care. What is good care?
• Keep it out of direct sunlight when not in use.
• Rinse off salt water.
• Suspend it for storage as opposed to laying it down.
• Alternate between strapping it face up and face down to transport it.
• Minimal dragging over cement

As with anything we purchase, the more you spend, the higher the quality. Fortunately with regards to kayaks, as little as $200 amps up the quality of the boat. The difference between the cheapest of the cheap and an elite kayak is about $400.

How much can you afford to spend?
Usually cost is everything but if you are a summer warrior, and live where summers are three months long, even if you can afford an elite kayak spend those hard earned dollars on other things and purchase a less expensive boat. But if during those three months you will kayak as much as a Floridian would in a year, it would be worth it to get the higher end kayak. Then again, if most of those paddles take place in a lake with little chance of scuffing the bottom of the boat, this would be another reason to not invest in an elite kayak.

The best time to purchase is at the end of season sales. Recreational kayaks take up a lot of a store's floor space and managers want them sold. Prices come down as much as $200 making it possible to purchase an elite kayak for the price of a non-elite!

Looking for a used kayak? Here in Nashville, many whitewater boats appear on Craigslist but recreational kayaks listings are few. Paddlers marry their boat and give them up only after they are beyond repair. I snapped up a rec boat within hours of the owner posting it on the internet, meaning it is possible to find a deal but if waiting to purchase a used boat is holding you back from paddling, rent or borrow until the end of the season sales. The most expensive types of kayaks are touring and whitewater. Some whitewater boats cost as much as $2000 and more.

TIP: Before purchasing a kayak, consider the size of the paddler and check the boat's minimum and Maximum weight limit suggested by the manufacturer. Height matters, too. A six foot person in a nine foot kayak is like trying to cram a size eleven foot into a size nine shoe. Conversely, children and petite women fit nicely, and paddle more efficiently, in eight to ten foot recreational crafts. For children, I recommend adding and securing weights into the bottom of the boat. The additional pounds will assist them with stability and tracking.

When purchasing consider a boat with this type of built-in handle.

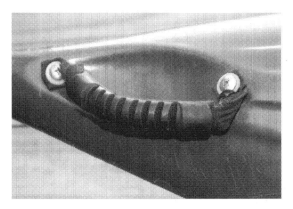

I've seen this type yank right out of the boat and there goes the means by which to carry it.

Nice features to have: Bulkhead, drain plug, cup holder, dry hatch, deck rigging, adjustable seat, foot braces, thigh pads, dashboard.

Special note: Of the 'Nice features to have" for recreational paddlers, the advantages of bulkheads almost puts it into the Must Have features, according to recreational paddlers without one. A bulkhead is an upright wall that reaches side-to-side behind the seat partitioning off, and sealing off water, nearly a third of the boat. Most manufacturers use the dry space to equip the kayak with a cargo hatch. When a boat swamps, the bulkhead prevents the stern from filling with water and provides greater buoyancy due to the trapped air which increases a paddler's chance of boat recovery.

Necessary Equipment

Paddle – The things to consider before purchasing a paddle are preferred waterway paddling, size of the paddler and width of the boat. The right paddle for the job is as important as the choice of kayak. If you are unsure, borrow other paddles. Finding out what you don't like is as valuable as finding out what you do like.

Paddle variables include length of the shaft, width and shape of the blades, and total weight of the paddle. Whitewater paddles are the shortest in the paddle family, independent of the size of the paddler. The blade on a touring paddle is narrower than the blade for recreational paddling. Recreational blades come in a variety of shapes and sizes.

Wide blades provide greater acceleration because they have more surface area to create water resistance, meaning that they are muscle builders. If you plan lots of river runs, select wider blades. If you plan on long trips, such as expeditions, go for a thinner blade.

Paddle weight matters! The cheapest paddles are the heaviest and quickly fatigue even seasoned kayakers. Paddle manufacturers are catching on that women need a smaller diameter shaft which saves female hands from blisters. I bought four paddles before I found the one that suited me best. One of the four was an expensive carbon paddle that weighed as much as a dime.

OK, a quarter. But the blades flexed during strokes and I couldn't go fast so I went back to hard plastic.

Occasionally we see bent shaft paddles. They look like the crankshaft of a car. Another rarity is a wooden paddle. These untraditional paddles are great conversation starters.

The average shaft length ranges from 180–220 cm. Tall paddlers or wide boats may require a paddle shaft length of 230-240 cm.

Keep the small rubber rings called "drip rings" a few inches from the paddle blade. Their purpose is to prevent water from dripping on the blades down the shaft of the paddle. If the drip rings slide too close to the middle, the water drips onto you; too close to the blade, they cannot do their job.

Even experienced yakkers mistakenly paddle with their paddle upside down. If you paddle with blades of an asymmetric shape such as in the photograph on the following page, ensure that the blade's scoop (also called power face) and manufacturer's name faces you. Most manufacturers print their company's name on the side of the blade facing the paddler, and most print it such that the print lies horizontal to the shaft. If the company's name is upside down so is the paddle.

A scooped blade works better for moving a kayak. Again, think water resistance. And last note, get a paddle that you can separate into two pieces. When the wind picks up, with a push of a button and a twist, you can "feather" the blade to slice through wind.

Gloves – There are two ways to paddle which we'll cover in Chapter 8 but if you are like most folks, you'll pull on the paddle instead of push especially if your background is canoeing.

You can tell how someone paddles – if they wear gloves, they are a 'pull' paddler (pull and push strokes are covered in Chapter 8). Pulling strokes cause blisters which is why gloves is in the required section of this text. Paddler gloves are made to get wet and cover only one-third of the length of our fingers. Velcro straps them securely around the wrists. To prevent mildew, toss the gloves in the washer with your laundry. If paddling during cold weather, wear full-fingered gloves made of neoprene.

Dry bag – A dry bag is a must. Two small ones are recommended over one large; the small are large enough to hold everything I carry including a digital SLR camera. With a boat moving swiftly downstream, there simply is no time to dig through a large drybag.

Note: The thick plastic transparent ones, in my experience, do not last as long as the vinyl ones.

What goes into drybags on a paddle? Standard things to keep in the drybag: Sunscreen, insect repellent, poncho/raincoat, knife, lighter or waterproof matches, first aid kit and anything that might be unrecoverable in the event of a capsize such as car keys, wallet, glasses, etc.

Take a change of clothes and put them in the second drybag or an airtight plastic bag. Store the clothes in the dry hatch if the kayak has one.

TIP: Purchase a drybag made of a bright color such as yellow or red. The dark blue and green ones can be difficult to spot when someone capsizes.

PFD – Purchase a Type III Personal Flotation Device with a generous cut to the armholes and shortened back designed for paddlers. Nice features to shop for: 'women's' cut for ladies, mesh for summer, neoprene for colder months.

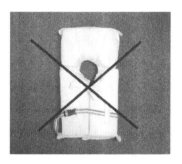

Summer PFD   Neoprene for winter

Do not buy the U-shaped ones typically seen on motorboats. They the wrong type for paddlers. Make sure the PFD is adjustable and correct size. Some use the standard S, M, L for sizes, some utilize chest size. Try it on before you buy.

Imagine someone grabbing you by the shoulder strap. Make sure that the PFD fits snug and that shoulder section is 'grabbable' without you slipping out from inside of it.

Whistle – Attach one end of the whistle to a lanyard or string and the other end to your PFD so it will always be available in the event of a capsize.

TIP: If using string measure the distance from waist to mouth, and add a couple inches for knots. This length prevents it from potentially wrapping around the neck while in the water. Also, please do not attach anything else to the outside of the PFD. Precious time can be lost fumbling through dangling belongings when grabbing the whistle during an emergency.

River shoes – For waterways with sandy bottoms, flip flops work. If on waterways with rocky bottoms wear waterproof shoes that Velcro or tie. Better yet, get yourself foot gear similar to these for summer - neoprene inserts prevent rocks from slipping inside.

These for winter paddles:

Sporting good stores sell a variety of foot gear for paddlers, the most humorous ones have individual toes much like gloves for your feet. As with any sport, fads come and go. It takes only one rocky river in tennis shoes to make you head for the nearest sporting goods store after the paddle.

Bilge pump – Even without a capsize, water manages to find its way into kayaks. It may dribble down the paddle, drip off wet shoes or the result of a fun water gun fight. If it rains during the paddle, that wide cockpit on rec boats permits lots of rain to get inside. Or you may run into a Class II section of the river and take on some water from a wave train.

Something as simple as a sponge takes care of small splotches, but every paddler must carry a device of some kind that removes water quickly and more efficiently than a sponge. The best one is pictured. As this device removes water from the inside of the boat it simultaneously pumps the water out over the side of the boat. When a boat flips in the water, even boats with drain plugs retain some water that must be bilged out.

Optional Equipment

Dog leash – Old paddler's trick for portaging the kayak. When the water is too shallow to paddle or there's an obstruction too dangerous to paddle through, clips the leash on the boat's handle on the front or back to pull it.

Seat pad – Recreational kayakers spend hour after hour in the boat. Unless the kayak has a padded seat, bring along some extra cushioning.

Tendonitis braces – if needed for elbow, wrists.

Paddle floats ("outrigger") – like training wheels they stabilize your kayak. Used for rescues or to create a carry-all kayak.

Wheels - for portage. These cradle one end of the bottom of the boat on foam rests while the other end of the boat is pulled by the grip. When not in use the wheels fold together and stash under the cockpit or deck rigging.

Wetsuit – Although listed as optional equipment, wetsuits (or the more expensive dry suit) is a must during cold months. Most people will not paddle during cold seasons but if you are a diehard paddler, purchase a wet suit called the Farmer John or Farmer Jane. These resemble overalls.

Normally we do not wear the same type of wetsuit that divers utilize. The full sleeves of diver's wetsuits chafe armpits after hours of paddling. At a thickness of 2-3 mm you'll stay warm except in extreme cold weather in northern states where 5 mm thickness is recommended.

In addition to the wetsuit, purchase wicking fabric, wear layers and absolutely no cotton anything. Cotton is made to keep the skin cool, an antithesis to the goal of wintertime paddlers. On top of the wetsuit, wear a splash jacket. These jackets have a gasket at the neck and wrists, the most vulnerable points of entry for water.

TIP: Wetsuits are unforgiving with regard to size. If your chest is forty inches, purchase a wetsuit made for that size; even if you could zip up a suit made for a thirty-eight inch chest, a deep breath would be difficult. Zippers at the ankles is a very nice feature to have.

Note: Some paddlers use the "Rule of 100" to decide whether or not to go out during cold weather. If the combined temperature of the water and air total 100 or more, they paddle. How to find out water temperature? Call an outfitter associated with that waterway. For instance, Google "kayak rental" and type the name of the river. Please note: if the sum of the water and air temperature add to less than 120, a wetsuit is recommended.

Chapter 5

How to Load and Unload

Women especially avoid kayaking due to the impossible act of lifting a boat overhead, or worse, purchase a kayak based primarily on its portability factor. While I sympathize and understand the rationale, and it is entirely reasonable, the trade-off of buying a lightweight, low cost boat is a less than ideal kayak that may put you at added risk on rivers. However, I applaud these determined ladies and will explain how to transport a long and heavy kayak.

For convertible owners, here's an amusing option:

Jessica Ely

When drivers and people along the road stare, extend your fingers, press them up against each other, raise your hand in the air and gently turn it back and forth in the Queen Elizabeth wave and smile. Seriously, do this at your own risk.

To enable one person loading a kayak on the top of a car, it is essential to have a secured rack of some kind on the car's roof. Racks can be secured foam pads, inflated thick plastic tubes or any other stationary apparatus, device or object.

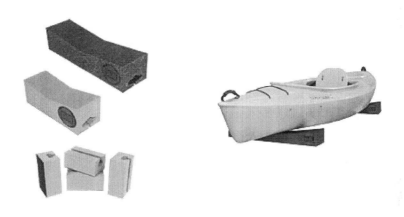

If racks pre-exist on the car, purchase a 'noodle' – the Styrofoam floating devices. Cut two sections and slit them lengthwise. Slip each piece over each rack.

At sporting good stores, a rustproof and durable kayak carrying systems is a bit costly at $400 yet lasts for years. They do not have to be removed when going through most carwash sites. J-shaped rack systems are popular – these require that the boat be lifted overhead to be cradled inside the crook of the upright J and are not recommended for women.

J-shaped rack system

If your vehicle comes equipped with racks, consider purchasing boots (also called "saddles") for less than $100.

Boots/saddles for pre-existing car racks

An entire rack and boot system costs over $400. These come with a key and impossible to removed short of a blow torch (read: theft proof). Most car wash facilities permit these racks.

What follows is a description of how I loaded a twelve foot kayak on top of a Mazda 323 for eight years: Pull the boat such that the front of the boat is directly beneath the middle of the back fender. Put a towel on the back of the trunk. Using the built-in handle of the boat, pick up the front and rest it on the top of the trunk. During the loading process, that is all the lifting that is required.

Photo by Jay A. Heath, Ed.D

Next, walk to the back of the boat and with a steady push, slide the boat first past the rear window and then between the boots/saddles, or on top of the protective device you use, centering the kayak over the length of the car. Walk a little distance away from the car to judge whether or not it is truly centered.

Unloading the boat is as simple as loading. Give it a tug to get it started. When it starts slipping down the back of the car, guide it as it slides down. Be sure to again put a towel over the trunk where the boat rests against the car to prevent scratching the paint. The maximum size, especially if your car is a compact, is fourteen feet.

Some paddlers transport their boat upside down to prevent it from buckling. If the boat is of sufficient thickness, transporting it right side up for a couple hours will not damage the boat. If the boat is lightweight, alternate right side up and upside down each time it is loaded. If traveling cross country, turn the boat upside down.

Next, how to strap the kayak down. For rack owners, there are a variety of straps available. I use the 2" straps with a slide-through clasp buckle on the end. They come in a variety of colors.

Photo courtesy of
David Quist Photography and Strapworks.com

There is another kind of strap with cinches that ratchet down. They are difficult to learn but once you get the hang of it, they are preferred by many paddlers.

Open the driver's door and step up onto the car facing the car. With one end of the strap in hand, loop it through the stable metal rod on the rack and toss both ends of the strap all the way over the boat to the opposite side of the car. When tossing, be careful with the buckle and the windows. Two straps go on the boat – one in front of the cockpit and one behind it. Open the back door (if you have one), step onto the car and repeat the process. If utilizing foam blocks and loop it with no rack system, follow these same directions.

Walk around to the other side of the car. Grasp the end of the strap that does not have the clasp around the metal rod on the rack. Thread this same end through the clasp buckle like this:

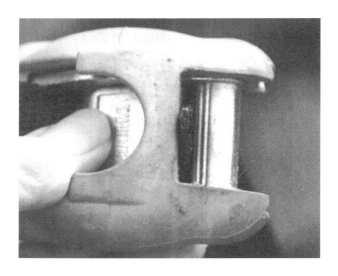

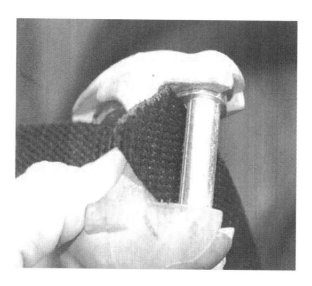

Next, turn the clasp buckle upside down and wrap the end of the strap around the rest of the strap three times.

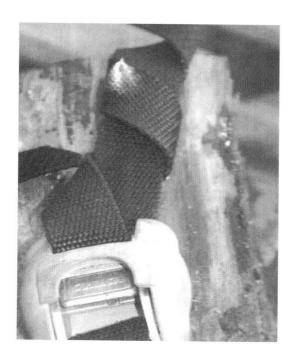

Insert the end of the strap through the loop closest to the buckle. Starting at the top, slide the trio of loops down toward the buckle. Repeat this process twice.

 This end piece was shortened for demonstration. When the boat is secured and unmovable, place the end piece in the open door and close the door.

Eventually, it will tighten to the point that you cannot pull anymore. Stop there. Repeat the process with the strap around the back part of the kayak. This time, pull down using both hands to get that strap as snug as you can make it. Go back to the first one and see if it will now tighten down any further.

Last, grab the side of the kayak and give it a good shake. It should not move. If it moves, you must tighten the straps. Any movement of the boat must be eliminated even if it means undoing the knots and pulling down harder on the straps.

For car owners without a rack and using some other type of cushioning device, especially if there is only one cushioned section of the kayak: Toss the end of the strap without the buckle over the kayak. Climb over the backseat and pull the strap through the inside of the car. Pull that end of the strap through the buckle and tighten it down as much as possible. Unless using the crank type strap, see the above description for knotting it.

Tie down the front and back of the kayak through the handles to underneath the front end of the car and under the trunk. Both ropes must be as taut as possible. So tight, that when you grab the boat and attempt to shake it, the whole car moves.

Dan Gislao

When paddling with others, watch how they load and strap their boats down. Some even have racks that crank up and down with a long bar that swivels down horizontally to the middle of the windows. The boat is placed on that long bar and then cranked up to the roof. This is the least labor intensive but most expensive system.

The first few times you load your boat allow yourself plenty of time so that you arrive on time for the paddle. Or load it the night before.

Chapter 6

How to Organize a Paddle

You are the organizer and today is the day of a shuttled paddle. The twenty attendees are a mixture of ages and experience levels. Its summer, the forecast indicates no rain verified with a last minute check, and everyone borrowed, rented or owns a boat. First we'll go over the details that led to this moment, followed by the details that follow it.

Note to attendees: The work behind a well-organized paddle is transparent and reading the details might help toward understanding occurrences that may or may not make sense in the moment. Also, the details that follow are based on my experience leading paddles that include experienced and inexperienced mostly adult paddlers.

For the following paddle presume that the organizer is experienced and that there is a pre-appointed safety person who knows the Universal River Safety Signals (which will be discussed in this chapter).

Before the Day of the Paddle

Mr. or Ms. Organizer, you've chosen to paddle on a Class I river. Considering that several attendees are inexperienced paddlers, rather than a ten mile stretch you'd choose for a group with lots of experience under their PFDs, you choose to do a six mile run. I strongly recommend that inexperienced paddlers do no more than six miles their first couple times. Given an average rate of speed downstream at two miles per hour, you add an extra half-hour for lunch and another half-hour for breaks. This calculates to four hours of river time. With a group this large, and that this is a shuttled paddle, add another hour for getting cars and boats where they need to be.

Most put-in locations, such as riverbanks and bridges, have no physical address. To avoid lost drivers, choose a brick and mortar physical location near the put in at which to meet. For today's paddle, that physical location is a gas station.

TIP: Some people travel by personal navigator, others by written directions. Posting the address of the gas station takes care of those traveling by personal navigator. When advertising the event, include a detailed list of roads and turns for those who travel by description navigation. Share your phone number with the group.

Unless the put in and take out are familiar locations, before the day of the paddle drive from the gas station to the put in and then to the take out, taking note of the length of driving time and miles. Scan the parking lot at the take out to ensure it can accommodate the number of cars.

One of the most frequent questions asked of a paddle organizer is, "Do you know what time we will get back?" There is only one correct answer: No. It's been my experience that behind that question is someone who needs to get back home on time to do something else later in the day. There's an old saying that applies – you can plan the event, but not the outcome. Your paddle today may be uneventful or full of surprises. That's what makes each paddle an adventure!

If there is any question about the quality of the run – perhaps it stormed a few days ago – check the internet for an outfitter that services the river. Type the words "kayak rental" and the name of the river as search terms. Call that river's governmental water management organization with any concerns. Did the storm knock down trees? What is the current today? Also, get the number of the county or closest city's emergency medical professionals and store it in your cell phone.

My group members sign releases on which they note their emergency contact. Most of my paddlers are frequent flyers; at home I maintain a spreadsheet of each one's emergency contact. A hard copy of that list gets tucked inside a plastic baggie and stored in my drybag. Ask everyone with a cell phone to store an ICE (In Case of Emergency) number. If their phone is password protected, either ask them to remove the protection for the day of the paddle or double check the spreadsheet for their emergency contact.

Request that every paddler bring: A change of clothing in a sealed plastic bag, lots of water (no alcohol), snacks and lunch, sunscreen, hat, sunglasses, bug spray, whistle, first aid kit, medical alert/medications/special need items. Please note: Ask anyone with special needs to please share that information with you.

Another frequently asked question is what to wear on a paddle. So much depends upon where you live, the season and time of the day of the paddle I can answer in only the broadest of terms. If the paddle is during a warm month and early in the day, recommend wearing layers – jacket, thick button up shirt, T-shirt and, if it is really warm, a bathing suit. Any type of wicking garment works, whether it is pants and/or shirt. I prefer wicking long pants that either roll up or button to convert into shorts.

Given the nature of the sport of continuous sitting in an upright position, to avoid a paddler tan wear sunscreen and re-apply after getting wet.

The Day of the Paddle

Ensure that your cell phone is fully charged. Keep it close because you will get calls. Load up and head out a half hour earlier than the departure time of the others. You asked everyone to meet at the gas station at 9:00 a.m. It's now 9 a.m. but one person is missing.

What happens next is up to you, yet here are my guidelines: If I do a headcount and someone hasn't arrived and hasn't called, at 9:05 we caravan to the put in. If they call saying that they are stuck in traffic, we wait a reasonable amount of time. What is reasonable? My choice is, if, by 9:30 they have not arrived, I call them with directions to the put in and head out. Sometimes organizers have to make tough calls.

Lead the cars to the put in. Remember not all drivers are speed demons, which is tongue in cheek for saying that some drivers rarely go over 45 mph. It's better to go a little slower and not lose anyone. Hopefully the jaunt to the water does not include many turns or red lights. If so, be especially cautious. You may want to assign a driver to bring up the rear and swap phone numbers so the two of you can stay in touch in case of stragglers.

It's my personal preference against caravanning cars on the highway. I found it too dangerous for drivers who, in order to keep up with the group, weave in and out of traffic. If you choose to highway caravan, give hard copy directions to each driver.

After all arrive at the put in, it's important that everyone helps each other unload boats and gear. The idea behind this goes beyond basic courtesy. It begins setting the attitude among the group for taking care of each other.

After everyone is done, and before anyone gets in their boat, it's time for the pre-paddle talk. Gather them in a group, and try to ensure that all are present. Sometimes it is like herding cats – they are excited and ready to hit the water. Introduce yourself to the group and thank them for coming. Ask everyone to state their name for three reasons - it makes for a better day when participants know the names of the others with whom they paddle alongside, it helps break the ice for those who are shy, and if the worst happens (a capsize) knowing names assists with communication.

Especially for the sake of the newbies, here are the things to cover while everyone is rounded up together:
• Briefly mention the highlights of today's paddle – river classification, length of paddle, stop for lunch on the riverbank, and any interesting things you'll pass on the river such as a waterfall, unique rock formations or animals.
• Safety – If one is pre-selected, introduce the safety person who explains that often we cannot hear each other on the waterways and that is why we use Universal River Safety signals to communicate.

If the point (or anyone else) raises their paddle and points to the right, the group is to paddle to the right side of the river. If someone directs to the left, go to left. Emphasize the direction in which the paddler is pointing is the direction to go.

Waving an upraised paddle three times side to side, or three long blasts on the whistle means emergency.

Raising a paddle overhead and/or extending both arms and waving three times means, "Stop now!"

If someone points their paddle straight up it means go down the middle of the waterway.

If a paddler makes eye contact with another paddler, points at them and pats their head, it conveys, "Are you all right?" To indicate that all is OK, the other paddler pats their head in response. If there is no response pat, the first paddler comes to the rescue.

If leading a group of children, turn learning these signals into a game: Line them up one behind the other and as the point conveys various signals, the children act them out.

Everyone must wear their PFD during the paddle.

• Now for the scary part. Ask for two experienced paddlers to volunteer to be designated rescuers. Explain to the group, and be emphatic, that in the event of a capsize you, the sweep and these two will be the only ones to swoop to the rescue. All other paddlers should clear the area and stop along the riverbank to wait until all is clear. Instruct them to retrieve personal items floating downstream if they can safely do so. Capsizes are not a rare occurrence and its best that everyone knows beforehand what to do.

• Assign the point and sweep paddlers. The lead paddler of the group is called point; the last paddler of the group, sweep. I recommend bringing waterproof walkie- talkies, they go into the hands of these two paddlers. Often, canoeists attend paddles with kayakers. If an experienced canoeist attends, ask them to do point. Canoes sit higher up in the water for better advantage to see downstream. Your strongest and most experienced paddler is the sweep. Whether conveyed with humor or stern warning, emphasize to the group that it is their job to stay between the point and sweep.

Note: The point kayaker stops progression down river if the group gets split. Staying together is that important. If the group continues to split, pull everyone over to give slower paddlers time to catch up.

• Ask newbies to identify themselves. Either ask experienced paddlers to buddy up one-on-one with a newb or assign buddies. On every paddle I've organized, experienced paddlers have stepped up to the plate, bless their hearts.

TIP: If today's paddle includes more inexperienced than experienced paddlers, before heading down river, take a few moments and get everyone in the water for a paddling lesson at as small a ratio as possible of experienced paddlers to newbies. If there are fifteen newbies on today's event and five experienced paddlers, assign four newbs per experienced paddler to teach the basic four strokes: forwards, backwards, turns and stop.

Last piece of the pre-paddle talk: Ask who drives the largest vehicles and, of these drivers, if they'd be willing to shuttle drivers from the take out back to the put in. Again, every paddle I've organized results in generous offers to assist. With a group of twenty, two to three vehicles are needed to return drivers to the put in. Request that all the other drivers to please give these two or three volunteers a couple bucks for gas.

Passengers stay with the boats at the put in while drivers follow each other to the take out. It's worth mentioning to the passengers that they should not put their kayak in the water until you return. At the take out everyone parks their car and then pile into the largest vehicles to transport drivers back to the put in. At the end of the paddle, someone returns these volunteer drivers to the take out to retrieve their boats.

TIP: After everyone parks at the take out, and before driving off for the put in, do a key check, meaning ask the drivers to double check that they have their car keys.

Note: Some paddlers prefer to drive first to the take out, place boats onto the largest vehicles and transport boats and paddlers to the put in. I think it's easier to transport drivers only and not boats from the take out to the put in.

Things an Organizer Must Have on Hand

In addition to the items mentioned previously such as sunscreen, water, etc. organizers must carry additional equipment and supplies. Everyone should have their own first aid kit but the truth is they don't. Make sure yours is stocked and that the case is waterproof. There are marine first aid kits.

I carry oral and topical Benadryl in my drybag. Realizing that oral Benadryl makes one sleepy, don't hesitate to administer it if the allergic reaction is extreme. If hives break out around the victim's neck and face or their tongue swells, administer Benadryl immediately.

Hand sanitizer comes in small containers and is invaluable if needed. Don't depend on dipping your hands in the river to get them clean.

Sporting good stores sell ropes specifically for water rescues. On paddles, ensure that five of you have a safety throw rope – the point, sweep, two rescuers and yourself, and know how to use it. Practice on dry land. A quick way to stuff the rope back into the back: hang the sack over your shoulder while pulling the rope toward you and cram it in. It doesn't have to be neatly coiled in the bag. When throwing it to someone in the water, toss the bag slightly upriver and allow the current to drag the rope to the person. Always dry the rope after the paddle and discard old ropes.

I keep a piece of rope tied to the handle on the back of my kayak. Attached to the rope is a big hook that has been used to latch my boat into the crevice of a rock mid-river during a rescue, to secure my kayak to a branch on the side of the river and to hook my boat to another one to pull it out of a jam.

As mentioned previously, purchase at least one set of waterproof walkie talkies. For larger groups, purchase two sets. Give them to the point and sweep; the extra set to the rescuers in the middle of the group. Before the paddle, ensure that all the radios are set to the same channel and subchannel. Cell phones do not always work on the river and the walkie talkies may be your only means of communication. Carry extra batteries, too.

Available at most drugstores are instant freeze packs, great thing to have on hand for injuries. With a hard whack, the inside container pops open and freezes the contents. Conversely for winter paddles, carry instant warmth packs for hands, toes and feet. If someone flips, gets cold and starts shaking, place the warmth packs under the victim's armpits, on their neck and both sides of the lower groin. For more information on what to do for hypothermia, please either research the subject or, even better, take a first aid class.

It's a good idea to carry an emergency blanket no matter what the season or where you live. These are no more than a large, thin sheet of shiny metal-coated plastic about the size of a shower curtain, yet folded up tightly in a plastic sleeve that requires very little space. I've seen paddlers make it through a capsize with a late reaction of shock. Wrapping them up in the blanket reflects their body heat back at their body. A new paddler may be traumatized witnessing their first capsize and should be monitored for shock, too.

Other things I carry for a day trip: Extra water, rope, glucose tablets, spare PFD and a snake bite kit.

Voice of Experience

If you plan to lead paddles, take a wilderness first aid and CPR class. Not only will it empower you with the knowledge of what to do in the event of an emergency, your commitment to safety will inspire confidence among the group.

Many capsizes result from a lack of confidence, meaning it is possible for a paddler to lose heart in their abilities. I am not suggesting that capsizes can be avoided simply by paddlers talking themselves out of it; capsizes often occur in an instant. Yet there will be occasions when capsizes can be successfully fought against. A paddler's confidence in themselves, their organizer and the group provide additional elements of safety.

It is not a question of whether or not a kayaker will capsize. It is a question of when. Some paddlers say we are all between swims. An organizer, however, will be held to a higher standard by the group. Do not lead paddles if you are a frequent swimmer. It is not amusing for the leader to be the one who needs the most rescues on a run and it could be downright dangerous. The group needs to know they are in the hands of a competent paddler.

There seems to be some sort of group psychology that when one person flips, in the moment others follow suit. I've had as many as seven boats flip at one time.

Organizer, you must have the ability to stay calm in an emergency; nothing contributes to that ability as much as experience. Please do not begin your kayaking years as a group leader. Move up through the ranks much like any other life event that requires skill. First be a proficient, strong paddler and then volunteer to point, sweep or assist as a rescuer. After that, lead small groups and build to larger ones.

Emphasize to the group that in the event of an emergency, there will be only one voice of authority – yours. Fear deafens people. Stay assertive. During moments of panic and confusion, it can help save someone's life.

Of all the unpredictable events that occur on a paddle, organizers can influence one of the root causes of many capsizes: fatigue. Watch for these signs:

• Someone asks how much further, and keeps asking.

• A paddler complains that their boat keeps going either to the right or left. It might mean their arms are giving out.

• A paddler falls behind. I had a paddler who insisted she preferred to paddle slow. There really are paddlers who prefer a slower pace but before this particular lady kept falling behind, she'd kept up with the group. Her sudden change of 'preference' concerned me. We switched boats. It was her bad tracking kayak that was wearing her out.

• Inefficient and weak strokes, different from earlier strokes.

• The paddler's body starts rocking forward and backward with each stroke, as if they were rowing. It means they are attempting to utilize the rest of their body to compensate for depleted arm strength.

• A couple miles into a run, many paddlers fall into a pleasant and serene paddling 'zone.' However, if someone becomes quiet with a facial expression of grimacing or intense concentration, they are fatigued.

• The most obvious – someone keeps complaining about being sore.

Cognizant that what happens to one happens to everybody on a paddle, if even one person shows signs of fatigue, pull the group over for a break. Odds are that if one person is fatigued, others are, too. If I suspect that the reason for fatigue lies more in the mediocre quality of the boat rather than lack of strength, I switch boats with that paddler. Words cannot describe the difference between paddling in a quality vs inferior kayak.

As mentioned some folks just prefer paddling slow. For them, paddling is more about getting away from it all than a form of exercise. Rather than hold back the whole group, I let them lag behind with the condition that the slow paddler has a buddy. When I reach the take out I note the time, and then wait for my cruisers.

As organizers, it is our responsibility to ensure that everyone is accounted for at the take out. Count the boats at the put in and take out. If your group is of a large size, plan separate runs or slow cruisers and faster paddlers. Another option is a put in time, for example, at nine o'clock for cruisers and ten o'clock for the faster paddlers with an organizer, point, sweep and designated safety paddlers for each group.

Unless the current or river geology will not allow for pulling over, we always stop for lunch. It gives everyone time to stretch their legs and take a pit stop. If someone needs a pit stop during the run, ask someone to buddy up with them and move the group slowly downstream until they catch up.

Drinking alcohol during a run is a sensitive subject. Even though I do not allow drinking on my paddles, adults imbibe without permission. The danger lies in an impaired ability to act quickly and appropriately. On a paddle, each of us relies on everyone else, whether it is giving a heads up about a submerged log barely under the surface, scooping up floating belongings after a flip or to blowing three whistle blasts on someone's behalf. It is as important for me to know I can rely on you as it is that you are sober and in control of your boat. If the problem persists, as organizers we have the right to say who is and who is not allowed on a paddle. That said, there exists camaraderie among paddlers. I don't know if it is the influence of leaders that set the tone or the result of similar traits among water lovers.

Organizer, hand someone their paddle after they climb in their kayak and give them a push off the riverbank. If someone is standing around while others need assistance, ask them to help. Keep that sense of taking care of each other first planted when unloading boats and gear at the put in. It is especially vital during times of need. The group must understand through words and deeds that they are dependent on each other until the end of the run. Discourage Lone Rangers, paddlers who gallop off from the starting gate and are never seen again. Again, you have the authority to decide who can, or cannot, attend your paddles.

Special note about children: For their first couple times out, children might think its fun to play bumper boats. We've paddled with an experienced eight years old past the game playing phase. Paddling with her is a joy, yet we still keep a close eye on her when the water gets challenging. If I were a group leader of children,

I'd discourage them from banging each other's boats until lunch time and then let them play. Enjoy your lunch while keeping a close eye on them. Emptying a kayak of water is hard work. If the children let the boats flip, let them help empty them.

Chapter 7

Oops!

Nothing scares newbies more than capsizing. We cannot eliminate capsizes, but reduce the risk - yes. In this chapter we'll discuss the most common and innocuous flips to the most dangerous, how to enhance paddling safety, describe a capsize moment by scary moment, and end with river protocols.

Most flips occur getting in and out of a kayak. It happens to even the most experienced kayakers. On one run, a paddler traversed twelve miles uneventfully then flipped at the take out. Nothing got hurt except his pride.

Kayakers learn from experience and that of other paddlers resulting in regional ways of doing things right. To use an analogy, in Florida after a hurricane that knocks out power to red lights, drivers treat each intersection as though it was a four way stop. No one formally broadcasts that practice; drivers learn it from one another. If power gets knocked out in another state, they may do things differently. The same applies to kayaking. Each region owns different methods of doing things right. Other ways exist on how to do things, how to enter and exit kayaks for instance. What matters is how well the method works. Here is the sequence I teach students to minimize flips upon entering a kayak:

• If possible, the kayak should be in water to behind the seat meaning about three-fourths of the boat is on water and one-quarter on land, and pointing toward the river.

• Place the paddle on the ground next to the boat. Either your buddy hands it to you after you are seated, or keep the paddle within reaching distance. If the paddle is in or on the boat and the kayak accidentally flips as you enter it, the paddle floats downstream. Not a pleasant way to start a paddle.

• Place a foot in the center of the kayak in front of the seat. It is important that you plant your foot dead center.

• Lower your body. The closer you are to the boat when entering the less chance of the kayak rocking.

• Twist your torso toward the boat and commit to plopping into the seat. By commit, I mean no hesitation during the action of your butt making contact with the seat. Hesitation means flipping.

• Bring in your other leg.

• Stretch your legs out and sit up straight. The more evenly your body weight is dispersed, the greater the balance.

• From there, either ask a buddy to give the boat a shove to launch it or scoot your hips forward to self-launch.

To recount, the sequence is one leg, butt, and then other leg.

Another method of getting in without flipping the boat involves bracing the kayak with the paddle under the coaming behind the seat.

Leave one of the blades on the ground for stabilizing the kayak.

To exit:

• When approaching land, paddle hard and fast to launch the kayak onto solid ground. Ideal for exiting means three-quarters of the kayak is grounded. At least part of the boat should be in water.

• Plant one foot on the ground, *lean forward* and grab the coaming on both sides of the front of the boat.

• As you lean forward, shift your weight to the leg on the land and exit. Ask a buddy to hold down or straddle the front or back of the boat until you feel confident getting in and out.

Another common source of capsizes involves getting perched midstream on a log. The worse thing to do is sit still. In almost every scary situation on the river, the absolute worst thing to do is nothing. You cannot balance the boat in a precarious situation for long. Hopefully your paddling buds are nearby and extend their paddle for you to grab while they pull. Regardless, start scooting the boat forward as soon as you get stuck. Don't scoot to the side! Keep making little quick jerks scooting *forward*. If you can safely do so without losing balance, stab your paddle against the obstruction to gain purchase while scooting.

Another frequent capsize situation – ducking under branches or anything hanging over the water. Lean forward or backward, not to the right or left. If you lean to the side, the boat will surely dip and then flip to that side.

One of the most challenging situations I've encountered is a boat trapped on a rock ledge. If stuck pointing downstream, it fills with water and becomes so heavy it cannot be moved. As soon as you realize your boat is grounded on a rock ledge, put one leg outside the boat to push off the rock. If the boat swamps meaning it fills with water, abandon it and get yourself to safety. It's up to the group to dislodge the boat with ropes and manpower if possible.

Another similar situation is a boat on a rock ledge turned sideways to the current. Again, the boat swamps but even faster than pointing downstream because the broadside is open to the current. Don't try to walk the boat off the rock. You do not want to go over the front edge of the rock sideways. If you cannot scoot the boat forward off the side of the rock, abandon it and swim to safety. Again, rely on paddling buds to rescue your kayak. The order of importance for all rescues: paddler, kayak, equipment.

One of the most dangerous conditions on rivers for recreational paddlers is strainers. They are called strainers because, as the downstream current pours through the pile of branches and tree trunks, the strainer sifts the water clean. I've seen the current flowing into a strainer grab hold of a thirty-two pound, eight feet boat manned by a seasoned paddler. The boat was too small and lightweight. *Strainers* are the best argument for a longer, heavier kayak for recreational paddling. Unless you live where river beds have no drop in elevation, such as most of Florida, most likely you will encounter strainers. They are life and death situations for recreational paddlers.

Strainer on Harpeth River, Nashville, TN 2008

Same strainer turned monster size, 2009

If the rivers are elevated, the only way to safely manage the strainer in the second photo is portaging kayaks. Get to the riverbank upstream of the current rushing into the strainer and walk your boat around the mass. However, if you are ever in the unfortunate situation of getting caught in a strainer's current, for kayakers who own *good quality* kayaks here's what to do: As the current forces your boat toward the strainer, turn the boat sideways. Do not approach it bow first. The goal is to get your body close to the mass of debris. As soon as the boat comes to rest horizontal to the strainer, push down firmly on the hip and leg closest to it. In other words, lean the kayak into the strainer. Don't push down too hard with your hip and leg; if you do, the boat will take on water. With the boat dipped down on that side and the side presented to the current raised up, a paddler gains a few lifesaving moments of preventing the water from spilling over the edge of the kayak and into the cockpit.

Reach with both hands and grab the thickest branches in the pile of debris, continue to keep your weight tipped toward the strainer and then hoist yourself up onto the strainer. As your feet make contact, test that it will hold your weight. Do not grab for anything inside the boat. Nothing is worth more than your life. Climb across the strainer to dry land if possible.

What happens next depends on the circumstances – the boat may crack from the force of the current, or fill with water and flip. If your buddies are immediately on hand and can safely do so they can attempt to save the boat. An inexpensive kayak capable of bending by hand has no chance, and lessens the paddler's chance, of surviving a strainer. The force of the water will collapse an inferior boat potentially pinning the paddler inside of it.

To avoid entrapment in a strainer, keep a vigil eye downriver – bridge pylons frequently amass strainers. If the strainer lies around the bend (most strainers are on bends) you will hear the rushing current. It sounds like a waterfall. Usually the water on the far side of the strainer moves at a brisk pace, too, but much more manageable than the current flowing into the strainer.

Presuming that you always paddle with at least one buddy, go single file past the strainer. Others stay in place until the paddler is past the danger and into safer water. The first one in safer water stays put to be available in case anyone flips.

A strainer caught me by surprise. On approach the river split left and right with dry land in the middle of the riverbed. There were only two choices – down river left or right. On the side I chose, around the bend lay a strainer that traversed the width of the river. There was no turning back. Upon approach, I turned my boat sideways. After the boat came to rest parallel to the strainer, I leaned into the mass of limbs and branches and, abandoning my kayak, climbed up onto them. My buddies were watching, landed their boats on the dry bed in the middle and rescued my boat. It took three men to pass me hand-over-hand from atop the mass of limbs onto dry land.

Safety Begins Before Wetting a Paddle

Recognize and eliminate factors that contribute to capsizes. Here are several pointers to assist recreational paddlers from taking a swim.

The right boat length and weight: Presuming a river with a mild current of two miles per hour, we're going to apply a safety factor method simply called "450."

That number is derived by multiplying the kayak's length by its weight. For example, a ten feet, forty-five pounds boat is 450. This minimum baseline for safety does not imply a 450 is 100% safe. Nothing on the river is 100% safe. Numbers greater than 450 increase the boat's safety factor for recreational paddling. The ideal is 540-564.

Stop when fatigued – better yet, before: Few opportunities exist for many of us to build upper body strength. Add to that the fact that an untrained beginner's paddling strokes are less efficient and more energy consuming than experienced strokes. The result - weak muscles that are suddenly overworked.

We're independent, self-reliant people conditioned to not show pain yet if your shoulders burn after a couple hours of paddling and it appears that everyone else is fine, rest assured that others are hiding their pain, too. I am grateful, and happy to comply, when an inexperienced paddler asks to take a break.

Buddies: Best practice is four paddlers at a minimum. Safety classes teach that in the event of an emergency, one buddy stays with the victim while two buddies go for help. If paddling with a group, staying together is the best safety precaution. If someone lags behind for any reason, ensure a buddy stays with them. Friends do help friends stay upright - it might be a helpful nudge that dislodges your kayak off an obstacle, someone holding onto the kayak as you climb inside or a coach when facing a difficult chute.

Skill level matches river classification: He had a lot of experience, it was her first paddle. On a Class II no less. She was in good shape and athletic and I might have made the same mistake. While she caught her breath sitting on the bank after he rescued her yet again, he asked his now enraged fiancée, "Do you still want to marry me?"

Do not let anyone talk you into a run that sounds too difficult for your ability. Conversely, if your paddle leader states that paddlers must have experience for a particular run, please respect that advice. Attending a paddle beyond your experience endangers yourself *and* the group. Organizer, it is kinder to send someone home if you believe their experience is subpar for a particular run than to allow them to attend.

A good question is, when to amp up from Class I to Class II paddling? The quick answer is experience. The more complete answer is *recent* experience which interprets to ability plus muscles. If paddling regularly with a group, check with the organizer for their opinion and ask for a buddy if you get a green light. If your paddling history includes gaps of time, rebuild paddling muscles on a few Class I runs before attempting Class II.

Know the condition of the run: It's those earthquakes in California, summertime hurricanes in Florida or heavy rains during springtime in Tennessee that alter the landscape of our waterways. Ask experienced paddlers, they'll tell you where to go, what to look out for and what's changed on the river. If you just can't wait to get started, head out to more open bodies of water such as a lake that is less affected by natural occurrences and always take a buddy. Never paddle alone.

No alcohol: Newbies + alcohol = capsize. It's not a good idea for *anyone* to drink and paddle.

Match the speed of boat with that of the downstream current: When the river channel narrows or bends, the speed of the current increases dramatically. To maintain control of the kayak, start paddling hard and fast. Dig in! I've watched many newbs panic, and stop paddling. As mentioned previously, stopping paddling is the worse thing to do.

Organizer, this is the time to make your voice heard. Coach that panic-struck paddler – call their name and assertively order them to paddle. Keep it short and simple: "Kyle, paddle!" Especially when rounding a bend with a strong current, paddle hard to lessen the chance of the current grabbing hold of the kayak, shoving it against the riverbank and flipping it.

Keep the boat pointing straight downstream
The best position for going downstream is the front of the boat pointing downstream. That sounds obvious, and it is, but at times even a Class I current pushes a boat sideways. There is a direct relationship between kayak and current regarding capsizes: the more the kayak is against the current, the higher the chance of capsize. If a kayak gets turned sideways, that is the front and back point toward the riverbanks rather than up- and downstream, the kayak becomes a dam, fills

with water and flips. If the flow is turbulent and you feel it pulling your boat sideways, dig in with all the muscles you've got and fight to keep the bow pointing downstream.

It's not always best to flow with the current

If the current is relatively swift, such as after a recent downpour, bends become trickier to navigate. Going with the current under these circumstances is a poor choice. After a storm, the water slaloms through the bend of the river. For the recreational paddler, unless the boat is under good control, it will slam up against the riverbank and get pinned there. From experience, it feels as if someone is tugging down on the side of the boat. In seconds with the trapped boat horizontal to the bank, the water will flow over the edge of the kayak and flip it. If the bend is sharp, even without any recent rainfall, the same effect may occur – getting pinned against the riverbank. Again, the worst thing to do is nothing. As soon as the boat gets pinned, press your hip slightly down on the side closest to the riverbank to offset the pulling of the water on the other side. Alternate pushing against the riverbank with your paddle while scooting the boat forward.

The following picture shows the safest line to shoot to avoid the kayak getting caught in a strong current. Note the current pulling toward the small strainer on the left in the picture.

To paddle with the current in this case, the boat would be pulled first toward the strainer and then slung toward the right bank. Instead, follow the path as indicated with the arrow cutting across the current and then into the calmer section behind the strainer called an "eddy."

Generally, if the river bends to the left, paddle to the right of mid-river. Conversely, if the river bends to the right, paddle to the left of mid-river. With an S curve, as shown above, paddle straight down the middle.

Capsize!

No capsize is to be taken lightly but the worst that happens during the course of most recreational runs is that the paddler gets soaked, and may lose some personal items. This in no way makes light of a life and death situation such as getting pinned to a strainer. No inexperienced paddler should be on a river that presents such extreme danger.

For the type of waterways on which you'll learn, it is most likely you or a paddle mate will have a situation like this one: The capsize happened so fast you didn't see it coming. If your organizer did their job, assigned rescuers are already on their way. Until they reach you, as obvious as it sounds, come out from under the boat and come up for air. A newbie once panicked to the extent that I had to lift her boat from over her and pull her up. She didn't swallow any water but we sat on the riverbank until she breathed normal and calmed down.

I've asked kayakers what is their first thought when they capsize. Their answer: To grab onto their boat. That makes sense, to desire grabbing onto something that floats and that is the ACA's recommendation. Grab your boat if possible and either hold on to the back of it or wrap your legs around the stern. If the boat floated downstream before you could grab it, start swimming for land. If the current is slow, swim cross stream; if the current is stronger, swim at a forty-five degree angle downstream. The goal is to get you out of the water as soon as possible. If the kayak floated away and the current is too strong to swim against, stay with your toes pointed downstream and float. Your PFD keeps your head above water. One of the rescuers may throw a rope. A student asked me to mention that, as obvious as it sounds, grab the rope. Rescuers, do not jump in the water unless it is absolutely necessary to save a life. Staying in your boat keeps you in a stronger position to assist.

Finally you are out of the water and safe. What happens next: Paddle buddies retrieve your boat and anything they can safely grab that's floating. This is why a dry bag is so important. Not for the obvious reason that water cannot get inside but, when sealed, dry bags capture air inside making them flotation devices to retrieve your most important items (like car keys). Avoid dark blue or green dry bags; purchase a bright color which makes it easier to spot floating downstream or if caught in branches. Some paddlers clip the dry bag to the boat. While you catch your breath and calm down, others empty the kayak of water or, if you need to move and the swamped boat is nearby, assist with emptying the boat. That is why it's best to purchase a kayak with a drain plug. A kayak filled with water is heavy!

Trip leader, there is no mistaking the sound of a kayak capsizing. Words cannot describe it; you will know it when you hear it. As soon as you see or hear one occurring, blow three long blasts on the whistle. Your duty is first to the paddler in the water; let others tend to the kayak and gear. If you have not participated in rescues before learning to lead paddles, practice rescues under non-emergency situations.

Practicing your first rescue during an emergency is not wise.

If the swimmer reaches dry land before your arrival, ask the closest paddler to stay with them while you assist with rescuing the kayak. Resist the urge, and discourage everyone, from flipping the boat upright mid-river for the purpose of pulling it. It's my experience that helpful paddlers who upright a kayak mid-river and attach a rope to their boat to tow the swamped kayak get flipped by the weight and instability of the water sloshing throughout the swamped kayak. Instead, point the front of your boat up against the middle of the flipped boat. Using your bow, nudge the flipped boat to dry land. If a designated rescuer assists, one nudges the bow and one the stern.

Once the boat is at the shore, one of you beaches your boat, hops on land and grabs the empty kayak while the other maintains position of keeping the kayak in place. It is critical that paddles have one, and only one, leader. Chaos and panic during capsizes make it difficult for people to think clearly. Some withdraw and get quiet, some spring to action at the first sign of trouble, some wait and do what they are told to do. It is your voice that they have keyed into from the pre-paddle talk and it is your voice that stays calm but assertive.

After a capsize, I pull the whole group over for a break during which I visit with each person one-on-one. Sometimes a capsize aftereffect is shock – surprisingly, it may be one of those who witnessed the event. I ask each person how they are while I touch their arm, shoulder or back, and look them straight in the eye. Do they make eye contact and what is the look on their face? Assess skin color – normal, pale, splotchy? Are they talking normally, stuttering, or worse, not talking. I ask permission if they indicate they don't want to be touched. Some get surprised or embarrassed by their reaction. Inject some humor if it is not inappropriate.

In my experience, most recreational capsizes result in *non-traumatic* capsizes. Still, traumatic ones do happen. Hope for the best but please always be prepared for the worst. It is worth repeating, group leaders, take a river safety course, get CPR certified and have previous experience with rescues before leading groups.

River Protocols and Courtesies

As with biking or driving a car, kayaking has its own protocols. Some are rules and some are courtesies shared paddler to paddler.
• At the put in, everyone stays in place until the last paddler puts their kayak in the water.
• If you encounter paddlers coming upstream while you are traveling downstream, honor the same protocol as that of the roads. In America, downstreamers to the right, upstreamers to the left.
• It is no secret that kayaks traverse waterways faster than canoes. Most canoeists do us the courtesy of allowing us to pass them. If they don't it's OK to get around them. It amused me once to hear, "That does it. Next time we rent kayaks."

• When the point utilizes a Universal River Signal, paddlers convey that signal to the paddlers behind them until the signal message reaches the sweep.

• If someone encounters a potential danger such as a log barely under the surface, they tell the paddlers behind them. Again, the information is conveyed through the remainder of the group upstream.

• At lunch break, I use humor to help assist ladies with privacy: "Men to the left, women to the right because women are always right." It's corny but it works.

• When departing from a lunch break, leave nothing behind but footprints.

• If lake paddling, paddle in the motor boat section and do not paddle in areas designated for swimmers. When crossing a lake occupied with motorboats, stay close together for several reasons. It makes you easier to spot, gives the motorboats less to dodge and keeps you close enough to respond if someone flips.

• During rescues, hopefully there is enough communication such that members waiting it out down river know what is happening. If not, and you are one of those waiting, please know that the rescue will take as much time as needed to perform and you are doing the right thing waiting it out.

• Hug, or at least rub the arms of, someone who flipped and stay with them until their breathing is normal. The human touch goes a long way to calming them down. The organizer, or one of the experienced paddlers buddy up with that person for a while after getting back in the water.

• Tell your group leader if you have special needs.

• If you are fishing or taking pictures, it is your responsibility to catch up with the group.

• I discourage paddlers from taking pictures of capsizes. If we were pre-internet, I might feel different. As a courtesy, before putting photos where they are available to everyone (like bosses and coworkers) ask the photo subject whether or not it is OK.

• Cell phone usage detracts from the enjoyment of the day. Take a few hours to enjoy nature.

• If you see or hear someone capsizing down river from where you are, the rescuers may be so intent on the event that they forget to flash the signal to stop to those up river. Pull over or paddle in place until all is clear.

Chapter 8

Basic Strokes

Four movements every paddler learns to get started: forward, backward, turn and stop. Because learning is more by doing than reading, we'll cover tips to make your hands-on learning more effective.

First, know where to place your hands on the paddle. Center the paddle on your head and allow your hands to naturally spread out a little past shoulder width. That is the correct placement — hands a little past shoulder width. For novice paddlers, that is one of the hardest things to remember. During class, their hands drift closer to the center of the paddle. For demonstration, use a shower curtain rod or long stick of wood. Center it on your head and place your hands at shoulder width, or closer, lower it and pretend to paddle. The ends flop. Hands at shoulder width or closer provides less control and weak strokes. Now slide your hands past shoulder width and pretend to paddle. You can feel the difference - that is the power point. Also, novice and experienced paddlers tend to allow one hand to drift toward the center of the paddle while maintaining the correct position of the other hand. The result? A boat that keeps pulling to one side (the side where the hand is at the correct placement). If your boat keeps going to the left or right, check your hand placement. Some paddlers put waterproof tape on their paddle at the correct hand placement spots.

Boats pull to one side for another reason. It could mean the dominant arm is doing most of the work. To compensate until the weaker arm strengthens, do two strokes on the weaker side for each stroke on the dominant side.

TIP: When paddling for the first time, concentrate on proper stroke technique, hand placement and keeping the boat under control rather than speed. Mind and muscles are laying down the foundation for eventual paddling by instinct. Find an experienced paddler who does not have a history of frequent flips and ask them to buddy up with you if the paddle organizer has not already done so. Watch your buddy kayak, mimic them and let them know about any specific problems you may encounter. It is best to learn good habits from the first time in the water because once a bad habit is learned it is difficult to retrain mind and muscles.

Sit up straight and paddle using slight torso rotation. It keeps the boat in better balance and allows the body to engage core musculature. A slouching paddler uses only their arms and shoulders. If your shoulders burn, correct your posture - sit up straight and use torso rotation. Consciously tighten the muscles of your abdomen with each stroke while utilizing slight torso rotation. A paddler told me that kayaking works the entire body except for the legs. I think he's right.

Going Forward: Especially if you've paddled a canoe, your instinct directs to more vertical than horizontal paddling. In other words, you will have a tendency to direct the paddle blade close to the side of the boat and at a higher angle when performing a forward stroke. While kayak paddling isn't exactly horizontal, it certainly is more so than canoeing because kayaks sit lower in the water than canoes. In the photo below, note the angle of the canoe oars:

Anne Martin and Bill Kelsey

107

Mary Brace

These two photos of kayak paddlers
demonstrate the correct height and angle of the
paddle for efficient river paddling.

Sit on the floor and pretend that you have a paddle in your hands. With a slight torso twist, reach the blade forward dipping the shoulder slightly on that side and pretend to plant it in the water near your feet. Stop. Is your hand above your head? If so, that is the elevated angle of a canoeing paddle position. Lower your hand; the blade naturally extends out more to the side. This is the beginning position of a kayaking forward stroke. Follow through with the draw by twisting your torso and stop the draw just behind your butt. That is as far as the blade should travel until you pull it out of the water to next do the same sequence on the other side of the boat.

Tip: If you get wet while paddling, you are lifting the paddle too high. The water drips down the length of the paddle and then onto you. If your lap is wet, extend the blades out more to the sides when paddling. When in the water, for a few strokes watch the top edge of the blade pass through the water.

Presenting a perfectly vertical and flat blade to the water increases water resistance and engages the torso ensuring efficient paddle strokes.

Watch top edge of blade keeping it in this position throughout forward stroke.

The slightest angling of the blade as shown below decreases water resistance resulting in weak and inefficient strokes. Keeping the blade vertical significantly enhances paddling strength.

This much of an angle will produce far less efficient paddle strokes. Especially when fatigued, paddlers tend to let the blade slice through the water at an angle as shown above. The result is less forward movement simply because the paddle is not creating enough water resistance. It's best to take a break rather than to keep trying.

TIP: On a lot of recreational paddle blades, the power face side of the paddle is scooped. Ensure that the scooped side faces you. If the company name is printed horizontal to the shaft, make sure that the company name is right side up.

After a few paddles, may you experience what I call the "Zen moment." With increased arm muscles and a vertical paddle, it feels as if the water is pushing against the paddle, rather than the paddle pushing against the water, as though a hand is gently pushing against the paddle with each stroke. It's hard to describe but in time I hope you have that "aha!" moment.

Two Forward Paddling Methods

There are two methods by which to forward stroke: "Push" and "Pull." Pull utilizes the muscles of one arm. Push uses both arms. Which one is the more efficient stroke and propels a kayak faster? The two-handed Push stroke.

TIP: The two-handed Push stroke firms up the flabby muscle often found on the underneath side of ladies arms. However, if you have wrist or elbow tendonitis, do not do the two-handed push stroke as it aggravates tendonitis.

The Pull Stroke: Most of us naturally do this stroke. With the left paddle blade in the water at the beginning of the stroke, pull it back with the left arm. The right hand just goes along for the ride. On the reverse side, the right arm does the pulling while the left arm goes along for the ride.

The Push Stroke: Pretend to hold a paddle with the blade submerged in the water on the left side. Open the palm of your right hand against the shaft of the paddle. With a punching force, push your right hand straight out from your shoulder. Even pretending, you may feel a little tension of the muscles on the underneath side of your right, and more active, arm. When in the water, if you can paddle with an open hand, you are doing this stroke correctly. Also, if you utilize this method, you will not get blisters.

Regardless of the Push or Pull method, sit up straight, keep the blade vertical and engage the core muscles by rotating the torso when paddling.

TIP: To veer toward the right, paddle on the left side of the boat. To go left, paddle on the right side.

Going backwards: Hold the paddle horizontal to the water and twist from the waist toward one side. Just behind your hips, with the power face of the blade facing toward the bow, submerge the blade. Untwist from your torso while pushing the blade forward toward your knees. Keep the blade close to the boat while pushing it forward. When teaching this stroke, it surprises students that it takes less effort to paddle backward than forward. Some paddlers paddle backward for a long safe stretch on the river to work new muscles groups while giving other muscle groups a rest.

Turning: There are several ways to turn. If river

kayaking, the easiest turn is to simply put one blade in the water straight up and down while holding it there allowing the current to do most of the work. Another way to turn is to do several forward strokes exclusively on one side. A third way is to perform backward strokes on one side only. Yet another turn is to do a forward stroke on one side and a backward stroke on the other side.

A more advanced, technical turn is performing a Reverse Sweep.

Hold the paddle waist high, twist from your midsection toward the back of the boat and look in the direction you want to go. Keep the blade straight up and down. Plant the blade into the water close to the boat. Untwist your torso as you pull the blade forward in a wide arc. Keep the sweeping arm straight. Repeat on the other side. When paddling, you'll probably do a few on one side and then a few on the other side rather than a pure left/right, left/right. On a paddle, backing up often means going backwards *and* turning.

TIP: If the kayak is a twelve footer, when going around a bend on a river begin turning your boat sooner rather than later. New paddlers tend to wait until they are already in the curve of the bend before negotiating the kayak. Caught in the current, they end up on the far riverbank wondering what just happened. Especially when long boats start turning, it takes effort and distance to straighten them out. When you feel your recreational kayak veering off course, correct it sooner rather than later.

Stop that boat: There are several ways to stop – circumstances and current decide which one to use.

Dodge and stop: The boat in front of you suddenly puts it in reverse. It's OK to play bumper boats occasionally on recreational paddles but the current is fast and you'd rather not. Plunge the paddle straight up and down into the water using muscle to force it to stay locked in that position. Holding down the paddle on the left side forces the boat to turn and gets you out from behind the boat in front of you. Next, do quick, shallow backstrokes on both left and right sides of the boat. Presume that it is prudent for you to also avoid whatever caused the paddler in front of you to back away.

Stay in one place mid-current: To go past a strainer, boats must go single file which means staying in place while waiting your turn. If the current is strong for a Class I waterway, a continuing series of mini-back strokes straight out from your waist keeps you in place. If the current is not very strong, simply put the paddle with the blade erect first down on the right then on the left side, a series of flapping the paddle up and down.

Quick stop: For a really fast stop, raise the paddle straight up and down vertically and plant the blade close to the kayak by your waist. Hold it there even if you have to use muscles to force the paddle to hold in place. The more securely you set the paddle, the more effective it works as a brake. It will turn your boat and as it turns, quickly alternate to the other side. What you are doing is applying pressure against the current your boat produced from your forward paddle strokes; if you've been paddling fast you've built up your own little current propelling you forward - that's a lot of energy to work against.

Caution: If the boat starts tipping toward the side on which the blade is planted, quickly submerge the other blade on the opposite side of the boat or slap the broadside of the blade against the top of the water on the opposite side. This is known as a "brace."

Before moving on to advanced stroke techniques, please let me bore you one more time to reiterate – utilizing core muscles and maintaining good posture while paddling increases endurance, builds awesome muscles from shoulder to butt and enhances the effectiveness of your strokes. Paddling utilizing multiple muscle groups builds tone and endurance and ensures that the muscles you'll need during crucial moments will exist. Make a conscious effort during any paddle to build strength.

Advanced Strokes

Side draw: The purpose of the side draw is to move the kayak sideways.

• Plant the tip of the blade in the water.

• While maintaining a straight wrist, submerge the blade. Keep the blade straight up and down and pull it toward the side of the boat.

• While pulling the blade toward the boat with the bottom hand, the top hand pushes against the paddle shaft. Pretend you are wearing a watch. With the side draw done correctly, your wrist (the watch) will be directly in front of your eyes as seen in the next photo.

• Stop when the bottom blade is approximately six inches from the side of the kayak. The bottom hand is inches above the water and the

submerged blade is horizontal to the underside of the boat.

• Twist your wrist such that your knuckles move closer to the boat and then raise the blade. The twist of the wrist decreases water pressure against the blade. This twist of the blade is called a slice.

• Repeat the process.

It is not necessary to bring the blade completely out of the water when repeating the process. Laying the power face flat on the water puts it in the position to start the second side draw stroke.

When teaching this stroke, instead of the top wrist ending in a position where students look at their watch, their top hand holding onto the shaft often raises over student's heads. When the stroke ends with the hand over the head, it results in a power loss. It takes muscle to force the top hand to end in the position of being directly in front of the line of vision. The net effect of this stroke is using water resistance against the wide blade to drag the boat sideways.

The sculling draw also moves the boat sideways. Pretend that you are slathering butter on a slice of toast with a knife using a continuous back and forth motion. That back and forth motion mimics the movement of the paddle blade just beneath the surface of the water during a sculling draw. Unlike many other kayak strokes, the sculling draw requires flexible wrist movement. With the movements performed under water utilizing wide recreational paddle blades, this movement requires dexterity, muscle and practice.

When the blade nears the surface, rotate your wrists in the opposite direction and move the paddle toward the bow. To put it another way, draw a figure "8" under water with the paddle. The sculling draw is a slightly more powerful means to draw a boat sideways than the side draw.

A stroke to move the boat across the river is the "ferry". An example of when to use the ferry is when the current is strong and you need to reach the far riverbank. Turn your head in the direction you wish to travel and stare at one object across the river. While maintaining a visual on that object, do a forward stroke on one side. This results in the boat pointing at a forty-five degree angle. Do a continuation of forward strokes and as you do so, the boat ferries at that angle across the river.

23964270R00066

Made in the USA
Lexington, KY
29 June 2013